# A WAY WITH WORDS

A journey of poetry and prose from the Gilmerton Writing Group

Published 2015 by Pilrig Press, Edinburgh, Scotland



A CIP catalogue record for this book is available on request from the British Library.

ISBN 978-0-9927234-4-6

www.pilrigpress.co.uk

Printed in Great Britain

Cover design and art work by Sheila Corrigan

# ACKNOWLEDGEMENTS

This book could not have been written and produced without the support and guidance of so many people.

We would particularly like to thank:

Heather Muchamore, Community Learning & Development Worker

Jade Mooney, Lilian Williams, Kirsty Brown and the volunteers who help to run Gilmerton Community Centre

Sheila Corrigan for her cover designs and Tracie Boyle for the typesetting of them

South Central Edinburgh Neighbourhood Partnership Community Grants Fund for their support to publish this collection

Pilrig Press for their willingness to publish the collection

## CONTENTS

# FOREWORD

*'Writing is a process, a journey into memory and the soul'*

*Isobel Allende*

It is my pleasure and privilege to introduce to you this collection of new writing from the members of the Gilmerton Writing Group. Whether your tastes lay in short stories, poems or memoir; in the humorous, the poignant or the unusual, there will be much here both to entertain and inspire you.

It is often said that writing, and the reading of it, is a journey. The production of our anthology is the culmination of many journeys for all of our members! From the ideas, to the writing down of the words; from the (gulp!) reading aloud to the group, to the editing of the works-in-progress, we've supported and encouraged one another to believe we can write, and we believe we have something very worthwhile to share with you.

The book is loosely split into three sections: a general selection of our favourite stories and poems, some more short pieces written on the theme of 'The Journey' in which we began simply with two characters on a train… and finally, a few comments and suggestions on the craft of writing itself.

So, with that said, we warmly welcome you to take a few minutes and join us on our exciting reading and writing journey!

*Anne Hamilton (Tutor)*

*December 2014*

# Threads Of Nature

*Elizabeth Nallon*

Autumn's ever darkening ingress sharpens the air.
The woodland's withering canopy rasps and fidgets.
Dying leaves loose their grasp, flitting silently;
falling gently, deeply flocking nature's floor.

# Consequences

*Sheila Corrigan*

He hadn't really lied – had he? Been economical with the truth – yes. He hadn't been married before, that's what she'd asked him, his Rose, seven years ago, when he'd proposed. He hadn't meant to deceive her. The past was past, nothing to do with their relationship. But now…

Was it really just three days, Monday, since he'd received that fateful letter? That cold business-like letter from a French lawyer informing him that Helene, the Parisian amour of his student days was dead, that their daughter whom she had been raising, was now his responsibility. A thirteen year old whom he hadn't seen since babyhood. Religious differences and parental disapproval had parted them shortly after Aurelie was born. When he'd returned to Scotland, he'd initially sent cards and presents but stopped when each was returned unopened. Now his child was coming to him; would be on a plane on Sunday, four days time. How was she feeling? Did she speak English? How much French had he retained? How would he know her? Oh what a mess!

How was he going to tell Rose? What could he say to her? How could he expect her to understand? How would she and their five year old twin daughters react to a stranger coming into their lives? He remembered his mother's sayings: 'Troubles like chickens come home to roost' and 'Be sure your sins will find you out'.

'Oh mum, you were always right. How I wish you were here now to advise me, to help me.' His head was in his hands and as clear as a bell he heard her say, 'Honesty is the best policy, son. Tell Rose the sooner the better. She will be shocked and hurt but she loves you. She's a good person. She must have time, as indeed all five of you must, to adjust to and cope with this situation.'

Aurelie curled into her aircraft seat in a cocoon of wretchedness. Waves of utter loneliness and despair engulfed her. 'Ma mere, ma grandmere et grandpere sont morts. Je regrette que je ne suis pas aussi. Mon Dieu et Notre Dame de Secours Perpetual, prier pour moi.' She was leaving behind all that was familiar, going to strangers. Her heart was already broken, shattered into smithereens each a needlepoint of pain. Exhausted, inwardly sobbing, she slipped into a restless, uneasy sleep.

Rose stood a little apart from David in the airport arrivals lounge, her thoughts and emotions churning. What a week it had been. Her beloved had been behaving oddly, so quiet, moody and detached. She'd begun to wonder if he was ill or having an affair. Then on Wednesday, he'd shown her that letter. He had a daughter in France! All these years they'd been together he'd never mentioned her. Rose didn't know how she felt: angry, disappointed, betrayed, cheated – none of those and yet all of them and yes, relief that he wasn't ill, wasn't seeing another woman. Here, Rose was waiting to meet this stranger off a plane to take her into her home, her family. She loved David but could she do this – be stepmother to her husband's ex-lover's child?

David's feelings as he awaited the plane bringing his daughter to him, were also in turmoil. His hands shook, his head ached, his legs felt like jelly. Telling Rose had been the most difficult thing he'd had to do in his life. Remembering her ashen, shocked face, her tears, his tears, his sense of shame, his panic that she might leave him or order him out of their home, still stabbed his heart like icicles. She hadn't left him but was stood here with him as he held a notice – Aurelie LeClerc – to identify himself to his own daughter.

He recognised her immediately, so like Helene. Her petiteness and apparent poise, the long straight dark hair hanging partly over one side of her face in that old Veronica Lake style her mother had affected. A tide of tenderness swept over him, rendering him speechless, half paralysed. Their eyes met, those blue blue eyes and involuntarily he stepped forward and embraced her, realising too late his mistake as she stiffened in his arms.

What Rose saw was a slight, vulnerable girl in a severely

cut black coat which would have been chic on a mature woman (Rose just knew it had been Helene's) but it made this thirteen year old child waif like and fragile. Her face, white and drawn, taut with tension, trepidation and fear, wore the same expression David's had on Wednesday when he'd dropped that bombshell into Rose's nice, tidy life.

As Aurelie recoiled from David's embrace her hair swung back momentarily revealing an ugly livid scar down the left side of her face. Rose's heart lurched within her at this sight. With every mothering instinct rising to the fore she said,

'Welcome to Scotland, Aurelie. I am so sorry for your loss. You must be exhausted, shall we get you home, then?'

Aurelie who'd resolved to herself to speak only French, replied shakily, 'yes, please,' and took the hand Rose proffered while David lifted her suitcase from the luggage trolley.

Together they proceeded to the car, shivering a little in the cold damp air. Rose tucked a rug round her charge as she settled her in the back seat whilst David paid the parking fee. As he slipped behind the wheel beside Rose, they squeezed hands, their first intimacy of that week, united in caring concern for their precious, defenceless passenger.

# Walking

*Coreen Connell*

Walking upward and onward
over purple heather and bracken,
A difficult and relentless slog
through many a peat bog,
in trepidation of castellated ridges
with fear of fierce biting Scottish midges.
Views from the summit to admire
no further and no higher.
A celebratory dram to toast
Another bagged Munro to boast!
A last photo and the horizon to scan
before our rocky descent; that's the plan
Into the cool lush glen below
and in the distance, flies a crow.
Worried now as ahead, the sun sets
A race with time – hurry, hurry,
Down to the pub, we scurry!

# The Beguine of San Benito

*George Chalmers*

Every month, she stole brief seconds to stare from the Forbidden Window. Timing sin, in sixty second gasps of guilt. Once, she glimpsed a shimmering black-clad woman move stubbornly, head down, across a rippling horizon that floated above the baked roofs of San Benito. A goat, on hind legs, walked beside her, conversing earnestly. He wore a garish waistcoat woven from threads of human regret.

Fifteen years of stolen seconds had allowed her to memorise every chipped tile, one overlapping the other into broken shade. San Benito's ancient track resembled a dipping plank balanced on the apex of a distant red triangle. For a count of sixty, she watched a burdened mother trudge the road, as if bisecting a geometric mirage. The goat cast a sudden backward glance – she flattened herself against the cool safety of the thick stone walls. Then, in defiance, she dared to return his stare. She saw the road tilt on its axis as the figure slipped ever downwards.

The beguine felt compelled to return. Again and again, capturing snaps of orange hot tiles and milk blue sky. No human ever walked that uncertain line. Occasionally, the man-goat looked back motionless, as if noting her every peccadillo. From the sanctuary of the thick, cool walls, she returned his stare.

At night, she'd retreat to her cell and her cane. Tonight she would administer eighteen strokes to her exposed flesh. Though she had stolen only nine seconds that day, the Beguine of San Benito had much else to repent.

# Mine

*Marie Campbell*

It feels like the whole world is sleeping. It is calming, this sense of being alone in the world, with no one knowing where I am. If I were to go missing, they wouldn't know where to start. I always walk, even if it's still early enough for buses. I don't want to speak, not even about fares and tickets. And buses always have CCTV these days, don't they? I know there are cameras on the streets as well, but I am anonymous in my loose navy tracksuit and trainers, with my hair tucked up inside an old Nike cap.

I am nobody.

It's cold tonight, the white vapour of my breath leading the way. I know these streets just as they know me; an invisible hand on my shoulder steers me.

There are many routes to where I am headed, and this time, I walk away from home and down the back street. A skinny tabby runs across my path then stops to stare, but I don't slow my pace.

He could wake up at any time and realise I am gone. I have been slipping something I picked up at work into his drink on the nights I go out. Still, something could rouse him.

It's a chance I'm willing to take.

I hear a rustle by the garage ahead of me. Likely the cat, but

I can't be sure. I edge around the corner. A man lies asleep surrounded by bulging plastic bags, his bulky form dressed in what is probably his entire wardrobe.

Almost an hour has passed by the time I reach my destination. As usual, the houses are in darkness. No windows glowing with lamplight, no flickering from a wide-screen TV showing a late movie. I have spent a lot of time looking out for night-shift workers and insomniacs. Of course, one of them could change their habits at any time, but that's another thing I have to risk.

Her car is parked on the driveway. The small, silver two-seater I would have guessed she'd drive. I slip the string of keys out from under my sweatshirt and over my head. They are warm from my skin. My hand shakes slightly as I take hold of one of them and scrape the point slowly along the passenger side, from the back to the front. It's too dark to get a good look but I'm satisfied that the scratch is long and deep. I turn to leave.

This should be enough, but I want more. Instead of putting the string back around my neck, I walk up to the house and unlock the door. I tense, sure that an alarm will ring out at any second, but the house remains silent. The floor in the hallway is a spotless, gleaming oak. A huge mirror framed in dull pewter dominates the wall above a side table with a neat pile of post, and a selection of pens in a pot by the phone. I shake my head at the lack of coats, shoes and debris and rummage through the pens. One of them is a black Sharpie marker. I uncap it and press my finger against the glossy wet nib. Not like the dried up ones that litter my desk at home. A large canvas hangs further down the hall. It is one of those nondescript muted scenes. I take the pen and scrawl across it, then gather up the post and stuff it into my waistband. I put the pen in my pocket, then notice that she has left her keys in a glazed ceramic bowl on the other end of the table. I pick them up and leave the house. I'll drop them into a drain on the way home.

I make it home in forty-five minutes – a personal best. By the time I take off my clothes and stash the post in my bedside drawer, it's after 4.00am. He's snoring softly beside me, and just as I am nodding off to sleep, I momentarily think how grating that noise is.

When the alarm goes off the next morning at 8.00am and I drag myself from the bed, I find I am alone in the house. The half-empty cup of coffee he has left on the worktop is lukewarm. I take a swig from it as I prepare for the day ahead.

He is quieter than usual. There is a furrow on his brow and his eyes are dull and heavy. His face seems thinner, and the faint flecks of silver in his hair are more noticeable. He has to go away at the weekend, he says. A work thing. I nod and leave the room without a word. There's nothing else to be said.

I keep busy all day Saturday. Cleaning out cupboards, washing floors, tidying drawers. I go to the charity shop and drop off bags. All the while, my skin itches with impatience. I go through her mail and shred bills and statements. I fill in a loan application on her behalf and walk to the post box to send it off, along with a couple of letters on which I have scrawled 'Not at this address'. I watch nonsense on TV and heat up pasta that I have no inclination to eat.

At last, it's after midnight. The streets are never as quiet on a weekend but I know the best way to go. When I get there, I go straight to the door and let myself in. More post lies in the usual place, and next to it is a vase of velvety yellow roses. I head for the stairs, where the shiny floor gives way to thick, creamy carpet, then along the landing. All of the doors – and I count eight of them – are closed. I head to the one furthest away and find the room inside lined with glossy white wardrobes. A vast chest of drawers sits between them, and in front of the window, a dressing table with neatly arranged pots and jars. I picture her, in her muted creams and beiges, the sharp black suits, the skinny jeans and loose tops. This is where they are housed, no doubt in perfectly ordered rows. I leave the room and find the bathroom next door. Even in the dark, it gleams. Towels as thick as sheepskin are folded on a rack. A tall bottle of bath oil sits on the side of the tub, and the air is lemon-scented. I open the mirrored cabinet, hoping to find nail scissors, but instead, there is a pleasant surprise. A pair of long, pointed hairdressing scissors. I wouldn't have had her down as someone who cut her own fringe. But these are perfect.

Back in the dressing room, I click on a lamp. I am sure the pale light won't penetrate the heavy drapes, and I need to see what I am doing. I open the wardrobe nearest to me and finger a long, delicate blouse, almost transparent and clearly expensive. The fabric rips easily as I shove the pointed blades through its front. It's almost a shame to spoil something so beautiful.

She has a few similar items, so I pierce each of them. I work quickly, and in silence. In the top drawer are a selection of neatly folded sweaters and cardigans. She keeps her scissors sharp, and it's easy to slice off a few arms. I refold them and put them carefully back in place. She has four suits – two black, two navy. The scissors are becoming blunt now but I persist and manage to ruin the trousers.

There is so much more I could do here, but it's time I left. A noise stops me as I head for the door. It is a toilet flushing; not in the next room where I found the scissors but somewhere, behind one of the closed doors. It's impossible. She can't be here. She should be at The Royal Oak Hotel, in a luxury room, celebrating her birthday. I've seen the email confirming it.

My heart drums in my chest, loud and fast. I close my eyes and hold my breath for what seems like hours, then creep from the room and down the hall. I pause by the door which must surely be the master bedroom. Before I can stop myself, I've eased the handle down and opened it, just a crack. I can't help but look in. They lie there, sleeping. My lover and his wife. The pain in my heart is almost too much to bear. My face feels damp and clammy and I clamp my lips together until I taste blood, fearful that I won't be able to stop myself from crying out. I hurry down the stairs and out of the door. I rub my hands across my face and pull up my hood as I begin the journey home.

This can't go on. He will leave her soon, I know it. When she becomes so needy, clingy and panicky that he can't bear to be near her.

And then, at last, he will be mine.

# Freedom

*R. Briden*

‘Let go.’ Wind breezed.
‘I can’t.’ Leaf shuttered.
‘You will.’ Wind stirred.
‘I’ll not.’ Leaf squealed,
And hung on still.

‘Let go.’ Wind blew.
‘I daren’t.’ Leaf feared.
‘Why not?’ Wind tossed.
‘I’ll fall.’ Leaf rocked,
But hung with will.

‘You’ll float.’ Wind soothed.
‘I won’t.’ Leaf bellowed.
‘You’ll dance.’ Wind puffed.
‘I’ll dive.’ Leaf squeaked,
But hung until,

‘Trust me.’ Wind whispered.
‘You’re safe.’ Wind consoled.
‘You’re sure?’ Leaf queried.
‘I am,’ breathed Wind,
‘Together we’ll dance and thrill.’

‘I’ll bear you.’ Wind calmed.
‘Let go,’ he mustered.
‘Ok.’ Leaf shouted,
His hand held high.

Wind whistled, Leaf whirled.
Wind whisked, Leaf twirled.
Wind blew, Leaf flew.
Wind rustled, Leaf swirled.

The Sun beamed brightly
Shining on gold Leaf.
Wind whistled sprightly
Freeing up spun Leaf
Dancing gleefully to the ground.

# Emotions

*Sheila Corrigan*

Maureen had never had much of a relationship with her brother, and very little contact with him after she left home. Now, here she was, seething with resentment, on a train with him, on a journey that would take several hours. She was so churned up inside, afraid, and not knowing what to say to him.

Connor, watching, recognised her struggle. In an attempt at lightness he said, 'You haven't changed much, always late.'

She'd almost missed the train.

'You've not changed much either, still as critical as ever,' she acidly replied. 'I didn't want to come at all. You don't need me, you could have attended to everything yourself. I want nothing. No keepsake, I have those in abundance in internal hurts and scars.'

'Oh, little sister, I know and understand that you are resentful and feel neglected and ill done by. The ten year age gap didn't help us to bond together. I realise that you did not know our parents as I did. By the time you came along life had dealt them many hard knocks. Mammy's health was poor. I know she seemed to prefer me, to favour me over you.'

'Well she did,' Maureen interrupted vehemently.

'With dad being out of work so much after he lost the business, drinking and spending what little we had on his alcohol habit, mammy came to rely on me. Not just to protect her when he got violent but to protect you too and for the little bit of money I could earn doing odd jobs. I know she loved you very much.'

'Well I never felt loved, only afraid.' Maureen sniffed, tears in her eyes and voice.

'Perhaps this trip, pulling together, will be cathartic and bring about a healing and unity.'

'Hmph,' was her retort.

After a seemingly interminable journey they arrived and had to telephone for a taxi. It was dark, cold and raining hard. The house was as bleak as the weather. It was obvious their father had not cared for it, and it had been unoccupied whilst he was hospitalised. The same wallpaper, carpet and curtains were in situ that their mother had chosen years ago.

They both spent a sleepless, restless night and in the morning resolved to book into a nearby hotel. The weather improved, cold still, but sunny; the air fresh after the rain and the sea sparkling in the sunlight lifted their spirits a little. It also revealed the extent of the neglect. They decided to employ a local clearance firm and concentrate their efforts on any papers or personal effects. Neither of them had attended their father's funeral. Connor had been in New

Zealand and not known Maureen's whereabouts, so had phoned instructions to the funeral directors. Now they stood together, surveying the place that had been their home, each experiencing different emotions, unwilling to, uncertain where to, start.

'Let's go into the loft,' Connor suggested. 'I do recall after mammy died many boxes were placed up there.'

The loft was surprisingly clean and tidy and just an occasional cobweb decorated the joists. Most of the boxes contained china, crystal and bed linen but in a far corner, Maureen spotted a small trunk. She hunkered down and opened it, with the key left conveniently in the lock. It contained photograph albums and diaries, and wrapped in tissue paper, a baby's Christening robe of white satin and lace. A matching bonnet and tiny hand-knitted shoes were each trimmed with pink bows.

A gasping sob escaped Maureen as she realised that these must have been hers. Connor, alerted by her reaction, joined her. Together, their mother, through her albums and diaries lovingly kept, led them down memory lane. They wept in each other's arms; Maureen, for her misunderstanding and misconceptions of her mother's love and protection, and Connor for the long sufferance of his beloved mammy.

Brother and sister were united as never before.

# Life's Rich Tapestry

*Elizabeth Nallon*

'You're very quiet,' Mark said, giving Linda's hand a comforting squeeze.

She forced a smile. 'Is it any wonder?'

'Don't worry about it, it'll be alright.'

'I hope so, but I'm not so sure. I wish you'd told them before now. I probably wouldn't be so nervous if you had.'

'I'm telling you, it'll be alright.' he said.

Mark was ever the optimist, she knew that.

'How about coffee and a cake?'

She watched as he made his way down the carriage. So young; so self- assured.

'That's Pitlochry coming up,' he said, placing the cups and cakes on the table.

'About another hour and a half do you think, Mark?'

He nodded at her and grinned. She relaxed a little as the train reached the Cairngorms.

'What age is your mum?' she asked, breaking the silence.

'She's forty-three, but you know that already. The old man's forty-seven.'

Linda thumped his arm, laughing. 'At least he's two years older than me.'

Mark put his arm round her. 'I hope he doesn't take a

fancy to you too.'

Linda got more nervous the closer to Inverness the train got. All sorts of scenarios ran through her mind. The look of horror on Mark's parents' faces, the tension on the journey to their house. Embarrassing pauses in conversation. Linda felt sick. She shouldn't have come.

Her head swam as she got off the train. Don't faint, whatever you do don't faint, she willed herself.

'There they are,' Mark said, waving to the couple heading towards them.

'Mum, dad, I'd like you to meet Linda. Linda, my parents, Karen and Ian.'

Linda's head screamed. Ian. Ian *Smith*. Oh my god, it's Ian Smith…

Standing before her was her boyfriend's father – and Ian, her first love.

# The Journey Home

*Coreen Connell*

The two of us waited on the platform at Edinburgh's Waverley Station early one summer's morning.

'Have you got the tickets?' my Gran asked.

'Yes, Granny, I've told you already, in my handbag alongside my purse and I've also got the rucksack,' I replied.

'Here comes the train. We're looking for coach B; our seats are reserved, so there isn't any hurry, Gran.'

The steam locomotive drew up alongside Platform 4 then the whistle blew, before the train conductors began opening all the doors.

'Take your time and mind the step, Granny,' I said as I took her arm and led her onto the train.

We walked down the central aisle of the coach until I found our seats.

'Here we are, you sit yourself in beside the window. I think you should take off your coat and make yourself comfortable. We will be on the train for a good few hours.'

My Gran took off her hat and coat, and I added them to my pile of belongings on the shelf above our heads. She kept her handbag close. Ten minutes later, the whistle blew and the train moved off slowly and noisily. We caught a glimpse of Edinburgh Castle as the train pulled out of the city.

‘I’ve never been to the Isle of Skye. Your Granddad would have loved to have done this journey with us today,’ my Gran blurted out between sobs. ‘He was born there,’ she reminded me.

‘That’s why we’re going there today on this steam train service, and he is always with us,’ I replied holding her other hand. She nodded, drying her tears on the hanky that she held tightly in her fist.

The train ambled along heading north as we chatted. Noticing that the carriage was full, I was thankful that I had reserved our seats, enabling me to keep my promise. The urban landscape became more rural with every minute. We ordered a cup of tea and shortbread from the friendly steward, wearing tartan, pushing a refreshment trolley. The steam locomotive was a special; this was to be its last run before the diesel engine took over in the Highlands.

The train was now passing some of Scotland’s most dramatic landscapes: the Pass of Killiecrankie. the white stark castle of Blair Atholl. The train then climbed up the famous Drummochter Pass, the highest point of the British Railways – our ears popping – before descending into the fertile Spey valley. Here, the fields of green alternated with the bright yellow of the oilseed rape that looked ready for harvesting. The beauty of the passing countryside dominated the conversation with my Gran who remained mostly quiet. The train stopped for a while at the busy Inverness station.

Gran and I enjoyed a light lunch in the buffet car. The smoked salmon and oatcakes went down a treat. We returned to our seats and sat quietly looking out the window enjoying the wonderful scenery. The mountainsides were covered with a carpet of purple, mingled with the lush greenness of the summer grasses dotted occasionally with sheep or cattle. The distant hills became a blur as the train steamed onward crossing sparkling water courses.

We stopped at many stations, some were lovely and quaint with many planters of colourful summer bedding plants, mostly blazing marigolds and lobelias, and other stations had newly painted signs shouting out their welcome. My Gran had fallen asleep, snuggling into the corner of the window. I smiled to see her so relaxed.

The lush hillsides with their silvery burns gave way to the steep-sided rugged mountains of the Torridon Hills to the north as the train made its way alongside Loch Carron. We arrived at the picturesque village of Plockton after following the stunning coast. Plockton has the reputation of being the Caribbean of Scotland bedecked in palms thriving in the warmth of the Gulf Stream and giving us the first glimpse of the Summer Isles.

The train rushed through towering narrow blasted rock, certainly an engineering feat, allowing the train access to its final destination and the view of the Atlantic Ocean. Gran and I were awestruck with the beauty of the views ahead, that of Raasay and the Cuillins on the Isle of Skye. As the train arrived at the Kyle of Lochalsh, I said to Gran, 'Remember your handbag,' as I helped her on with her coat and made sure I had my bags. We disembarked carefully as I assisted Gran off the train. We followed the signs to the harbour that, thankfully, was within sight.

'Let's hurry, the ferry that will take us to Skye is there already, but be careful,' I called to Gran as we walked briskly towards the harbour on the mainland.

I had been dreading this short part of the journey as I am not much of a sailor but the weather was kind to us and there were no white peaks on the water. The rocking motion of the Caledonian Ferry was soothing rather than the cause of my usual 'sea sickness' and the fresh sea air blew in my face. My Gran held on tight and looked across the sea. We disembarked from the ferry and walked slowly towards the pier.

We stood at the end of the pier on the Isle of Skye with the Red and Black Cuillins watching over us as we carefully reached into the rucksack and took out the urn. We held it together, opening and scattering the ashes.

'Granddad wanted his ashes thrown to the wind and to be home,' I said to my sobbing Granny.

I held my Granny's hand as we called out in unison, 'Goodbye. Love you always.'

# Creatures of Habit

*Marie Campbell*

I stared at my reflection in the window as the familiar green fields flashed by. My skin was ghostly white, like the cotton wool clouds floating across the crisp blue sky. It was one of those perfect spring days; one of those days that should have been full of promise.

'Yes,' I could hear him saying. 'We make this trip twice a year, April and September. Regular as clockwork. You can get cheap tickets if you book far enough in advance. Creatures of habit, that's us.'

He made that little snorting noise that passed as a laugh. Not that what he was saying was even remotely funny. The woman sitting next to him was clearly itching to get back to her Hello magazine. No doubt she was silently willing her phone to ring and save her. I felt a headache stirring, just above my right eye.

'Don't we, dear?' He was talking to me now. 'I was just telling this lovely lady how much we enjoy our trips up North.'

I clenched the aluminium edge of the table until my knuckles were as white as its Formica top, and nodded. How was it that the word 'Dear', so short and simple, could affect me like nails on a blackboard?

He leaned forward and began to rummage in the hessian shopping bag he had propped between his sensible brown brogues. I had a sudden urge to rip them from his feet and hurl them out of the window. From where I sat opposite him, I could see the top of his head shining through the strands of greasy hair. White specks fluttered down and settled on the shoulders of the jacket that he insisted on wearing, even though it was, at best, fit for the charity shop. I felt faintly nauseous, perhaps from the motion of the train. Or perhaps not.

At last, he produced a plastic box and peeled off the lid, then held it out towards me. I looked down. White-bread sandwiches, with thick pink ham poking out of their sides.

I shook my head.

'Please yourself,' he said, helping himself and taking a large bite. 'Don't blame me when you're hungry later.'

I closed my eyes and tried to block out the sound of him chewing. I pictured myself at a restaurant table, with shiny cutlery on a pressed linen cloth, a proper napkin on my lap and a cool glass of white wine at my elbow. A waiter would appear and I would order my lunch from a leather-bound menu, not take it out of a Tupperware container.

'Where are you going?' he said, as I picked up my bag and shuffled across the empty seat next to me.

I licked my dry lips and rubbed my forehead. 'Toilet,' I replied.

‘You’d better be quick, then,’ he said. ‘We’re almost at a station.’

Was that even true, I wondered. That you couldn’t use a train bathroom when it was at a station? Or was it just another ‘fact’ from Gerry’s book of wisdom?

It didn’t matter now, anyway. I stood on the platform for a moment, holding my breath, until the train pulled away. I wondered how long it would be before he noticed that I was gone. I headed for the exit and instinctively walked towards the nearest bus stop. And then I raised my hand and hailed a taxi. Things would be different, from now on.

# Love Lives On

(For the anniversary of the start of World War 1)

*Sheila Corrigan*

We two shall never meet again
In happiness or sorrow
The day I prayed would never come
Is now my sad tomorrow

Our hearts were wrenched asunder
As you marched away to war
To face the brutal thunder
Of bombs and cannons roar

You toiled in the trenches
Plagued by fleas, rats and mud
Overcome by stenches
Of smoke, fire, death and blood

Know that I love you dearly
And your memory precious hold

Deep in my heart, my very soul
It never will grow cold

Dear heart our love will live on
In our baby yet unborn
I'll rear him with all the love
That you to me made known

I'll nurture him and treasure him
And tell him much of you
Yes, tell him, of you,
My love, his daddy.

# Nobody's Up There

*George Chalmers*

On a slick November night in the late 1950's we emerged from the La Scala movie theatre in Dundee. Somebody Up There Likes Me was showing and, though a cold rain stung my face, a warm glow kindled inside.

Crossing some tramlines, we turned into an alleyway leading to the top of our street. He walked ahead, paused at the side door of a dingy bar then moved on. I scuffed down a narrow flight of ill-lit stairs that opened onto a cobbled area. Even at four or five paces behind, his hard breaths were audible – quick bursts – as if to clear his nostrils. He turned up the collar of a leather-patched reefer jacket and swaggered on in loose-limbed fashion. I had trouble keeping up.

High, windblown lights illuminated parts of glistening dark cars. Ahead, a drunken man swayed towards us, his top half a couple of steps in front of his feet. Singing softly, he seemed unaware of our presence. I moved to let him pass. When he drew level, my father gave him an uppercut that sent him backwards as his false teeth shot upwards. He landed near a Ford Popular and began to groan. The man looked as old as my grandfather.

'C'mon you – get a move on,' barked the liberty-taker.

I stopped looking at a man who could have been someone's

granddad, to catch up with a person who could have been a father. But he wasn't able.

That is one of very few vivid memories of my father and I in company. The earliest is when, at six, I got us thrown out of Billy Smart's Circus. A clown tried to placate me from 'threatening behaviour' towards a whip-happy ringmaster. I attempted a few infantile right hooks and kicks to the shins of the yellow-toothed clown, but was ushered out of a secret flap in the Big Top, followed soon after by my father clutching a refund. Perfect for him. Not only had he fulfilled a reluctant commitment to take me out, he now had the entry fee for higher jinx in the local pub, plus the pint-magnet of a funny story to tell. An incident drunkenly retold, until eventually, I thought I wasn't there, as story merged into shifting realities.

A more positive memory is travelling pillion on a borrowed motorbike snaking back from Errol races. Aged nine and fearless, I stood swaying into every bend as we roared home to a cold-water flat in a rat-infested dockland. Apart from a controlled dive off a high board, it was the closest thing to flying.

Three other encounters bear witness to certain similarities in our character. Aged thirteen, whistling on the last lap of a lengthy paper round, he ambushed me in a tenement close. A smell of stale beer hung about him.

'Any tips?' he asked through a cloud of Woodbine.

'Aye, stay away fae the hoose,' I replied, surprising myself with a rapid reply.

He laughed. Next second, I'm down on one knee trying to refill empty lungs. He walked away. I sat on the stairs, gasping; the remaining papers were delivered whistle-free.

Three years later, came a rematch. In the mid-60s, Dundee had a vibrant, living city centre. When pubs and dance halls emptied, people congregated at a coffee stall, drinking weak tea and eating dodgy mince rolls. Depending where one stood, an allegiance to one of the various city gangs was openly declared. Crowded into the doorway of the Sixty Minute Cleaners, a quartet of us finished the evening with a nightcap of cheap wine.

'There's your auld man, George,' nodded one of my pals. I remember walking towards him and ramming my forehead into his face. He staggered back, but didn't go down, so I followed up with punches to his jaw and body. (Like he said, 'Hit them fast and often – if you don't knock them out, run'). In the heat of the moment, I forgot that last bit and two giant constables separated us. It was a split decision.

When the police discovered we were related, they shook their heads and said they had more to do than 'sort out domestics'.

'You don't get on wi' yir dad then, wee chap?' quipped one, looking at the damage to my suit. The other one laughed. I might have joined in if it wasn't for the vice closing round my ribs. 'You'll take him next time,' said the first.

At nineteen, his words proved true. On a fierce summer's evening, in a tight space between air-raid shelters, the pecking order got sorted out. A no contest in fact. It's sobering to beat up a man who figured prominently in those important formative years. An encounter that intermittently rings like a cracked bell. We had a relationship built on fear and I reinforced its pointlessness.

When he worked, he took lengthy trips on merchant ships sailing to faraway places. Not that life seemed calmer, only quieter. Edgy silences punctuated by Housewives' Choice and Saturday Night Theatre. Then he'd hit land again and another radio sailed out the window to crash in the backcourt.

After one trip to the States, he made it back with some money; bought a second hand, polished walnut radiogram from the local flea market. Scratchy 78's of Robert Johnson, Billie Holiday and Beniamino Gigli filled the single room. When the money and drink was gone, I watched as he reduced it to kindling with an axe. Unfortunately, Mailer's observation that Alan Ladd was just, 'A small boy's idea of a tough guy' arrived too late. He should have married the sea; the only companion whose dangers tamed him, for a spell.

He died, under a cloud, in 1984. The world feels no loss. That cold, sparse funeral. I've never shed a tear. It may not be too late to grieve, but some lack the will.

# Maggie's New Home

*Marie Campbell*

Maggie looked around the room. So this was to be her home for the rest of her life. She took a deep breath and eased her bones into the recliner chair. It was covered in red vinyl. Easy to wipe clean, she supposed. She stood, wincing as the familiar pain shot through her hip. Old age was grim. She made those noises that old people make when they've sat too long in one spot. She'd always enjoyed a lie in, when she was younger. Now, she was awake with the larks, adding yet more hours onto days that were already too long. She forgot things. Her bowels had slowed down and then ground to a halt. She hoped they had prunes here.

She stood before the tiny mirror. Her hair, once deep, glossy brown, and as thick as a horse's tail, was thin and almost transparent. It saddened her to see the pale pink scalp peeking through. She'd always loved to read, but now, finding the right pair of glasses seemed too much of a chore. She had her little TV though; she could keep up with the soaps. And she did like to hear what those Loose Women had to say, especially the mouthy blonde one.

She picked up a picture, framed in cheap fake oak, and smiled. The children. That was what life was all about. Not that she'd seen them for a while. And wasn't likely to; she couldn't see them trailing all the way to this place.

Maggie sat back down and closed her eyes. There was some sort of commotion along the corridor. She could smell boiled cabbage with faint undercurrents of piss and bleach. Not the best of smells, but she'd suffered worse. She knew she should try to stay awake; napping in the daytime meant she'd be up even earlier in the morning. But it would pass the time. It had taken her less than an hour to unpack her meagre belongings, arrange the pictures, put her few clothes into a drawer. And it was ages until teatime.

She started to drift off. She expected he'd be looking down on her now, having the last laugh. Or so he'd think. He'd always known how to wind her up, what buttons to press. But he'd pressed too hard, and too often.

Maggie hadn't thought about it really, just took her sharpest knife in her hand and shoved it deep into the soft mound of his belly. He hadn't suspected a thing as he lay there dozing, dribble glistening at the edge of his open mouth. She hadn't expected to end up here, of course. Not in a million years. But they'd made an example of her. Just because she was old, they said, didn't mean she should get away with it.

It wasn't so bad really. She'd been in prison most of her life. It just so happened that this one had thicker walls and more locks.

# My Whole Heart

*Coreen Connell*

As I slowly and purposefully run my fingertips
Down your cheeks over your enticing rosy lips
I desperately search for your inner soul
As we lean against the old brick wall
For my love and heart, I give thee
Without restriction or boundary but free

To walk along that sandy lonely beach
Always within my ever welcome reach
Hand in hand, then arms tightly around you
Waves crashing and islands in distant view
I yearn for you, though my heart in two may break.
Ever disbelieving – must pinch myself wide awake

Arm in arm, hand in hand, shoulder by shoulder
Friendship and love will not smoulder
Support and infinite care
I hereby, solemnly swear.

Desire and lust kept at bay
Unleashed when we're away

Believing whole heartedly – we are surely meant to be
Wondering if you know how much you mean to me
Brought together by good luck, fortune and fate
So deservingly of the long patient wait.
Your gentle soft touch is all too much
The future together is now within our clutch.

# Departures

*Anne Hamilton*

You told me you were leaving me as I did the Sunday dishes. I didn't stop. I could hear your breath behind me and picture your left elbow leaning heavily on the counter, your face red and wet with exertion. I didn't say anything. So you told me her name was Carmel, she was forty-two and that she understood you. It was a textbook departure.

'You've been a good wife and mother,' you offered; you could afford to be magnanimous. 'You will stay on here, of course.'

I scrubbed at a bit of burned Yorkshire Pudding and made a mental note to buy new scouring pads.

You floundered. 'For God's sake, woman. Always so bloody silent, so bloody frigid.'

Then you grunted as you hitched up your trousers and headed back towards the whisky decanter.

'Edwin.' I stopped you. 'How many women have you slept with during our marriage? Six, seven. Or is it more?'

'What the hell…?' You blustered.

'It's a long time, forty years,' I reminded you. 'I would have expected it to be more, that's all.'

Your self-righteous disgust led you into your new Mercedes S Class with the personalised registration plate.

I fumbled with the ties on my flowery apron and let it lie where it fell. I kicked off my sensible shoes to join it.

I had worn mini-skirts when I first met you. Flashing long legs, long hair and longer eye-lashes along the Kings Road. The basement flat in Belgravia had been a fluke: the landlord liked pretty girls and boys, and a quick fumble in the gloomy pantry every month covered the housekeeping. (An arrangement, if not venue, that has mostly suited you too).

The card appeared on a Monday in the summer of 1967, simple and white, embossed with a silver crest. It was the day my cousin Ailsa had spent begging me not to marry you.

'He's a bore,' Ailsa had said, pausing to blow a sexy cigarette smoke ring through pouting lips. 'A boring bore who will go through life blaming you because he's a boring bore.'

We drank too much that day, Ailsa and me. We lurched home arm in arm, falling over and giggling. I should have met you an hour earlier but I decided I didn't care. We found the card stuck on the iron-railings outside my flat. Ailsa leaned across next-door's Silver Cross pram to pluck it free.

'Oh God, you have to marry Edwin-the-boring-bore after all,' she had shouted, flapping it around. 'It's a sign. The boring bore is changing his spots.'

Scrawled on the card in thick black ink was: 'Your White Knight called… but you were out.'

She assumed it was from Edwin and full of wishful thinking, I let her. Later, alone and sober, I ran my finger over the insignia of the local laundry and kissed the handwriting. Don's.

Don, my soul-mate.

Don, who insisted I was out of his league…

That night I the double deed: accepted you and told my mother.

'I'll still be there for you, sweetheart,' Don had said as we made love the day before my wedding to you. 'All down the years, whatever it takes.'

He wasn't my only lover – when you, Edwin Robinson made me Mrs, I grew thoughtfully into the role – but Don will always be my only love.

What if it takes forty years? I wondered as I went upstairs to my bedroom and picked up my phone.

*What if it takes forty years?* I sent Don the text message, didn't bother to await his reply. I changed into jeans and boots; his cottage was in the middle of nowhere. I tugged off my wedding ring and laid it next to the urn containing my darling Ailsa's newly cremated ashes.

In the kitchen, I left you a cold salmon supper with a card alongside: *'My white knight called… and I was in,'* it said.

# Just Another Day?

*Elizabeth Nallon*

Tick tock, tick tock,
must get the washing done.
Tick tock, tick tock,
now hang it in the sun.

Tick tock, tick tock,
next prepare the lunch.
Tick tock, tick tock,
here comes the hungry bunch.

Tick tock, tick tock,
next vacuum our bedroom floor
Tick tock, tick tock,
what's that behind the door?

Tick tock, tick tock,
a lipstick case, bright red.

Tick tock, tick tock,
he's had someone in our bed.

Tick tock, tick tock,
the clock hands seem to slow.
Tick tock, tick tock,
how could he? My Joe.

# A Long Way from Home

*Coreen Connell*

My husband and I parked our red car off the main road just south of Tyndrum, Argyll. We had planned to climb the next two Munros on our tick list – Beinn Dubhchraig and Ben Oss. We set off on a fine sunny June morning to conquer both summits, our faithful hound running ahead.

The first crossing of the day was a traditionally stone built bridge over the swollen waters of the Fillan. It had been raining for days resulting in it being muddy underfoot but that did not deter us. The outline of the ridge of Beinn Oss was in view. Our track became less defined as we walked towards the pine forests giving us an awe inspiring view of the monster, Ben Lui.

The path became more boggy as we made our way to a burn that tumbled its way down and over huge boulders. The rain had turned the meandering burn into a mighty frothing and roaring small river. The walking books gave a descriptive route and suggested a small bridge for the crossing that was now within our sight.

I could see the old bridge was no longer intact – years of wear and tear and the inclement weather ensured it took a beating and there were more planks missing than remained. My husband jumped across in no time but unfortunately, I could not go any further. I stopped, looked and then looked again. I pleaded to my husband to find another way across but there was no alternative route. I stepped forward, inching my way across the planks, over the gaps where I could see the burn racing beneath and white water swirling over the rocks. I hesitated, again looking up to my husband.

'It is safe enough, I made it over without a problem,' he shouted across over the thundering cascades of water. I screamed for help; he drew closer and stretched his hand out and I, perilously and cautiously, leapt across the gaps.

We continued walking through one of the last of the remaining remnants of the great Caledonian pine forest before climbing steadily upward to the bealach between Ben Oss and its neighbour. We were amazed to see a pair of golden eagles soaring but, sadly, the weather was changing.

We reached the summit of Ben Dubhchraig in a few hours but visibility was almost nil and the winds were now near gale force. We kissed the cairn and placed the token stone on top before hastily abandoning the summit.

I was nearly blown off the top, the wind stealing my breath away, so with head bent low, hurrying along the descending route to the bealach. I shouted that we should abandon the second summit. Despite my apprehension and anguish, we continued but the weather worsened. The winds grew increasingly stronger and I was struggling to keep up with my husband. This normally did not worry me, accustomed to lagging behind, but that day the low cloud and wind driven rain was making visibility almost impossible. We reached the second summit within another couple of hours and again without the reward of a spectacular view.

The two of us huddled behind the cairn on the leeward side, grabbing some high protein biscuits and a drink before agreeing to go our own way down the mountain and not following the planned route. The deciding factor for me was that we would not have to cross that disintegrating dilapidated bridge and most likely in the dark. The clag worsened and we struggled to see one another let alone any landmarks. The GPS stopped working, and resorting to the map was a struggle as the wind and the rain whipped it about to a soggy pulp akin to papier mache. It was getting late and we were really concerned that we may not get off the mountain today. Neither of us were prepared for an overnight stay, no survival tent packed and already wearing all our spare clothes to keep warm. My husband was worried and said out loud,

'If only it would clear for a minute or two, so I can get my bearings as I know there are crags nearby. We will have to huddle here behind this rock as it too dangerous to go any further.'

Just then, as if Someone Above had heard him, miraculously, the fog lifted, and he shouted, 'Hold the map quickly,' as he opened it up against the wind.

The two of us pored over the map, aghast that the view in front was indeed a precipice and across the glen stood rows of pylons. Great, we thought, as the pylons are easy to find on the map but unfortunately, it also meant that we were on the wrong side of the mountain. We had a good bit further to walk to pass round the cliffs. My husband shouted,

'We will have to run, but carefully, as far as we can before the mist returns. We are heading over there, the lower we can get, the warmer and more sheltered it will be.'

Almost in tears, I started running and stumbling my way across and downward, worried at how high up we still were. My husband chose the route and I dutifully followed, thankful that the clag had not returned yet. He shouted that he could see the burn that we were to follow. He had been fishing in Strath Fillan years before, and knew that the gold mining industry had built a metalled road they could follow, once they made their way along the burn.

We continued to scramble for ages before the clag returned. Two hours went by, walking in the dark with our head torches guiding us in the heavy rain until we reached our car. I was in tears with relief but now ecstatic, finally to be going home.

# Whispers and the Hollow Heart

*Elizabeth Nallon*

Amy pulled the white, woollen blanket around her shoulders. The September sun had dimmed and the breeze chilled her wooden shelter. A thud and the chink of pebbles drew her from her thoughts. From the summer-house, she watched as a ball cascaded down the banking into the pond. Green and russet leaves, knocked prematurely from their young branches, followed, fluttering down, spilling outwards, in the circular ripples. Tears pooled in her eyes; Michael had planted that Acer.

In spring Amy had helped Michael build the summer-house, unaware that by summer it would become their sanctuary between Michael's hospital visits. By autumn he rarely had the strength to walk down the garden to it. When winter's icy grip took hold, Amy sat alone, warmed only by the heater that whirred at her feet, comforted only by the blanket pulled tight around her. Sleep that eluded her in her cold, lonely, bed crept up on her in the warmth of this shelter. The view from the summer-house became her view on the world.

Nine weeks and three days after Michael's death, Amy returned to work. She granted loans, processed mortgages and recovered debts. In June she resigned. The view from the summer-house again became her view on the world. On the worst of days she sat still, lost in her thoughts. When days were easier she tended their garden, her garden, weeding the borders, turning the soil, and mowing the lawn.

Today she sat hidden in the blanket's folds.

Voices drew her from her thoughts. A boy of about three came into view. His blond hair curled over his right eye, and his bottom lip trembled.

It steadied quickly, Amy noticed, at the sight of the ball bobbing in the pond like an apple at Hallowe'en. The child was followed by a tall, athletic looking man of about thirty.

Amy watched as the young man knelt, and with his arm outstretched, flicked the dripping ball onto the lawn.

'This is a nice garden; we could play football here, Uncle Simon,' the little boy said.

Uncle Simon's glance seemed to take in the garden, the lawn, velvet underfoot, and striped to perfection. Surrounding it, the terraces of floral spectators swayed in unison to September's chant. Their delicate petals of pink, purple, red and gold, their team colours.

'I don't think that's a good idea,' he laughed.

The little boy clambered onto the ornamental bridge. 'Come and see the fishes, Uncle Simon,' he squealed, all thoughts of the ball apparently gone.

'Come here, Peter, we should go.'

Amy sank lower in her chair, pulled the blanket tighter.

From the bridge the little boy glanced in her direction. He then turned and hurried towards his uncle. He whispered and pointed towards the little building, where Amy had retreated further into the shadows.

The uncle approached the wooden shelter cautiously, and knocked on the glass door.

Amy sat still.

He opened the door.

'I'm sorry, I had no idea you were in here,' he said to the fair-haired, young woman. 'I did ring the front doorbell'

'It's okay,' said Amy.

The little boy peered through the window, his nose and lips flattened against the glass. He squeezed passed his uncle and stood before Amy.

'Is this your house? I like it.'

Amy smiled.

Uninvited he clambered onto the chair next to her.

'Come here Peter, we should go.'

'I live next door,' Peter said. 'Me, and mummy and daddy and Buzzy,' he added, legs swinging frantically.

'Buzzy's the hamster,' Simon offered.

Amy smiled again.

'Susie's getting married today. Mummy said I couldn't go 'cause I don't like gravy.'

Simon laughed and shook his head.

Amy heard herself laugh too.

‘We’re having chicken nuggets and chips for tea,’ Peter continued.

‘And peas,’ added Simon.

‘I don’t like peas,’ the little boy stated.

‘Mummy said you have to eat your peas.’

‘I don’t like peas,’ his arms were now folded and his face overshadowed by a frown.

Amy suspected Uncle Simon had lost that argument.

‘Can we go now? I’m hungry,’ said Peter, shooting off the chair and out the door, stumbling in his haste.

‘Slow down,’ Simon called after him.

Amy locked the summer-house door and followed them over the bridge.

A little later the doorbell rang. She was surprised to see Simon and Peter again.

‘We wondered,’ Simon began, ‘would you like to join us for chicken nuggets and chips?’

A smile played on Amy’s lips and colour flushed her face; she giggled then asked, ‘is that with, or without peas?’

# The Kid on the Stairs

*George Chalmers*

During Dundee's hungry fifties, the 'kindness of strangers' meant more than the price of a bag of chips. Certain people became more significant than others in an ongoing, sometimes confusing, socialisation process.

'Nuthin' but whores an' comic singers,' slurred my over-qualified mother, a phrase that provided more bait for an already curious fish. One day in particular left its hooks embedded.

In a dimly lit flat, a truncheon's throw from the Sheriff Court, I stood silently immobile beside a man in a raincoat. Heavy curtains remained closed against the day. A dark, silver striped animal skin lay in front of a well-banked fire. Then a worn, overdone woman emerged from behind a kitchen door that folded in on itself. An aroma (now recognised as real coffee) followed her into the room. She approached me, holding out a blue-veined hand, limp with gold charms. I handed over a small canvas bag which she took wordlessly, emptying its contents of coins onto a metal tray. Chris, the man in the raincoat, removed his cap, rotating it in his hands. A back-lit display cabinet full of ornaments drew me towards it. Gentle tinkling of glass on glass brought a warning look from Chris that stopped me dead.

A huge, barrel-chested man unfolded himself from a sofa to scoop the animal skin from the floor, then slip snugly inside it. He walked past, leaving behind a whiff of fierce alcohol and picked up a hat with a black and white chequered band.

'I'll away and start my shift,' he said, ducking low to miss the door lintel.

The woman nodded. 'He cannae produce his helmet 'til he's in the street,' she said, separating the pancake of coins into neat ranks of similar value.

Chris sat beside her, smiling at something I didn't understand. He (the neighbourhood bookie) had shadowed me through town – past street-corner Teds, pubescent High School girls and distracted constables. He produced a notebook from his all-year raincoat then waited, until she'd finished sorting and counting separate piles of pennies, florins, half-crowns, shillings and tanners. They talked in numbers for a while and I panned the room. A polished radiogram stood near a small corner bar, made of bamboo. A female's breathy torch song worked its way into my bones. Coals, shifting softly in the fire glow, sparked and settled.

Back at the table, the woman double-checked each pile with a ripple of her thumbnail. They nodded to each other, saying the amount simultaneously, laughing, part of an old familiar game. She handed Chris an exact amount from the mix of coins piled on the tray.

He passed me another tanner. 'That's us square, wee chap.' He looked to the door, 'mind the roads on the way back.'

I hesitated, reluctant to quit the other-worldly atmosphere of the room. Drinking in again, the back-lit figurines, geometric mirrors, the wall lights shaped like shells and an unused companion set, gleaming gold in a spotless tiled hearth.

'Mighty fine place, Ma'am,' I said, shooting a line from some Western.

They burst into laughter, and the power of humour remained a possible way out of uncertain situations.

The woman turned, draping an arm over the back of the chair. According to local folklore, anyone who looked in her eyes was turned to stone. 'You're fae Gellatly Street,' she pointed, 'number 4.'

I kept my head down and nodded. She got up from the table and I took a wary step back.

"Do you want some juice?" she asked, eye-balling me rigid, 'then come with me.' She put a guiding hand on my shoulder, activating what hairs were sprouting over my body.

The kitchen was tiled in double-cream and pillar box red; gentle bubbling came from a shiny steel pot on a grease-free cooker.

'What's that smell, missis?' I asked, looking at the hour-glass shaped pot.

'That's the smell of Java when it's perfect," she replied. She removed the pot, placing it on a wooden chopping board covered in octagonal scorch marks that distilled the significant history of these people. Two small cups and saucers were set out nearby on a blood red Formica table top. She poured out a full tumbler of American Cream Soda that I finished in two gulps.

'Try not to be too much like your father,' she said in an odd warning tone and delayed action bubbles exploded inside my eyes, filling them with mock tears. Taking the glass, she moved to the sink, turning one of the taps. In a few seconds, after a splutter or two, hot water came from the tap.

Transfixed I said, 'you get hot water – inside your hoose! – how's that?'

She didn't answer, just smiled, running a red fingernail down my cheek, tracing boyish skin with intimidating tenderness.

Later that night, after the pubs closed, I regulated the gas lamp on my stairway for a wild-eyed woman.

'That's mah brother up there,' she warned some muttering men, 'so behave - right!' They peered round, trying to see upstairs. I shuffled into a dark corner. She knelt on her handbag. Drunken, grunting men laughed at each other, throwing coins onto the stairs as they left. I put the light full on and, when she'd picked up the money, she handed me a shilling. Sitting next to each other, her breath smelled of onions and wine; she offered me a Woodbine.

'Ah'm only nine missis, ah don't smoke,' I said.

She squatted on the communal stair toilet, leaving the door wide open. 'You're older than ye think, son.' Her laughter echoed round the tenement.

When she left, I bought a pie supper and mushy peas. Wolfed down, sitting on the nice warm toilet seat.

# Ed and Friends

*Sheila Corrigan*

Square, squat and sturdy
In his coat of brown
He welcomes all and sundry
With never ere a frown.

To all the waifs and strays
He gives a house, a home,
A safe place to stay
Where none are left alone
but enjoy hospitality
leisure and well-earned rest
Relaxing in pleasure
After each day's stress.

Spluttering and coughing
Slowly turning green
No respite in the offing
As far as can be seen

Sympathy stirring
For his incontinent friend
In wet pools standing
Abandoned and forlorn

Long prong fingered Jake
Exhausted and jaded
Lies alongside
Ben's blunted blade,
Mike, mowing machine,
Rose the hose
Trusty tools and handy stools
United soon will be

With plant pots and paint pots
And scented pot pourri
And much other jumble
Of chairs and spares
And bits more humble
Laden shelves
Old garden elves

Compost, screws and nails
And even fertilisers

Square, squat and sturdy
In his coat of brown
Ed the Shed
Welcomes, all and sundry
With never ere a frown.

# Neam

(an excerpt from a novel in progress)

*R. Briden*

The path ahead lured me curiously. I'd never been down there. As I followed it I could just make out the top of a large stone wall looming over the evergreen bushes. 'How odd!' I thought. 'It doesn't look like the ruins of a house. Maybe a wall to keep people out? But why is it so high?' It was about twenty metres long, and stood five metres high! The wall was overtaken by ivy and thick vines twisting and curling their way up. A strange tingling sensation swept over me. Hiding behind the tangled vine was a door painted dark green. It would take a bit of work to get to it, so I worked my way through the underbrush to the other side of the wall instead. There, was another tangled mess, and a field. Disappointed, I turned to walk away.

A rustle in the vines behind me made me jump. Looking right at me was the same chicken from yesterday. I knew because it was a very strange chicken, all white except for a single iridescent emerald plume in its tail feathers.

'I've seen plenty of chickens, but I've never seen any like you!'

The chicken clucked loudly as if in answer. I laughed as it

tilted its head to one side. To my surprise, the chicken turned and pecked at the door like a woodpecker, then turned to cock its white head again.

I chuckled. 'What do you want?'

It clucked, and making all manner of noises, turned and knocked on the door again, for that is what it was doing.

For the second time that morning I exclaimed, 'How odd! Do you want to go through, you silly bird? You could just go around.'

The bird ruffled its plumage and squawked louder than before.

'Ok! Ok!' So I fought through the mess of vines to get to the door. Reaching for the knob, I turned it and pulled. It opened a crack but not enough. The twisted vines were keeping it closed. I yanked hard and the chicken darted through.

Curiously I peeked around the door. My eyes widened, and that mysterious tingle washed over me again and made bumps stand up on my arms. I struggled back through the bracken and ran around the wall. No chicken. Just more bracken and a field. I rushed back to the door. On the other side, the chicken had turned and was staring at me from a dark forest.

Trembling, I squeezed through into the night and closed the door behind me. It made a strange click and my heart sank to my stomach. I tried the door. Locked! Nervously, I looked to where the end of the wall should be. There was no end. Not in either direction. I could feel the blood drain from my face. My eyes widened. The chicken had been joined by a dozen others of the same breed, and they were all looking at me. By some strange phenomenon, they all raised a wing and motioned for me to follow. There was really nothing else I could do besides sit down and cry, so I followed.

They led me deep into the woods. It was so dark I could hardly see them. Down, down, down we went into a gully and back up the other side. I could hear a stream rushing by and saw it reflect a glint of moonlight. The moon in fact suddenly became quite bright over the stream. The birds lifted their wings in flight to cross. As soon as the moonbeams touched them a strange metamorphosis took place.

Their wing span and necks became long and elegant. Not quite swans but not geese either. At least not like any I'd ever seen. A flock and flutter of mother of pearl and the emerald iridescent plumes glistened and gleamed. When they reached the other side they all turned as one to look at me. I knew they wanted me to follow, but I didn't want to get wet. Besides, I didn't know what that moonlight would do to me.

At my hesitation one of them flew back larger than life. I hadn't realised they had grown in size as well. As if by instinct I climbed onto its back and it lifted me in the air. Suddenly the stream was a river. Each bird rose to the air and joined us.

The climb was almost instantaneous. I had hardly even noticed the trees, until I looked down and saw them as far around as the eye could see. Absolutely no sign of my estate anywhere. I couldn't help but be awed at the brightness of the stars, or the freshness of the air.

As I clung for dear life we swooped and glided. 'What is this place?' I wondered aloud. 'Where are you taking me?'

'To Neam.'

As if things couldn't get any weirder!

'Who said that?'

Nothing. I watched the birds closely.

Miles and miles of trees passed under us. 'How am I ever to get back?' I thought.

'Trust me,' the voice whispered in my ear.

Terrified I slowly turned my head. No-one was there. 'How can you know what I'm thinking? And how am I to trust you if I can't see you and don't know who you are?' I said.

There was no other sound but the beating of wings. We flew for hours. My eyes became heavy from the air blowing in my face, and as if by some enchantment, I drifted off to sleep.

Next thing I knew I was in a soft bed of moss and lichen. Sitting up with a start, I groaned. My body ached all over from the tension of trying to stay on the bird. Slowly I began to take in my surroundings. There was a fire in a hearth in the middle of the floor which was made of roughly hewn planks. The walls resembled the frayed inside of tree bark. A dark red and green tapestry stained with soot hung over the opening in the wall.

'I assume that is the door,' I said to myself.

I stood to stretch my legs and went to investigate. The tapestry felt heavy as I pulled it back. Cold air swept over me, and the same bright stars shone in the night sky. I seemed to be in some sort of tower or something. Leaning out I looked up. High in the air was a treetop. I looked way down and pulled myself back in. It appeared to be an enormous tree. Something floated by. Then another. Snow!

'How can it be snowing in October?' I wondered aloud.

'It is not October here.' The voice chuckled.

Shivers ran up my neck and I fearfully glanced over my shoulder. 'Who are you?'

'You will know in good time. Watch and see my light rise.'

The sky held me transfixed and I could do nothing else. The horizon began to soften to a lighter and brighter blue, then pink and into peach before the orange globe peeked over the trees.

'The colours here are so vibrant,' I breathed.

'Everything born here reflects my light.'

'Whose light! Who are you?' I was getting impatient.

'You will see... in time....' The voice grew to a whisper and faded away.

I leaned out of the opening again. Not so far this time. There appeared to be a ladder made of rope leading all the way down. 'Should I go down? I don't know what else to do. I'm not sure I really want to wait for whoever owns this house to come back. This is all really freaky. I want to go home.'

But how was I ever to get back? What if one of those enormous birds lived here? They were the only ones I knew that could take me; that knew where to go. It only made sense that a house in a tree belonged to a bird. I decided to be brave and wait.

'What if he tries to eat me? He hasn't eaten me yet.' I encouraged myself.

*******

## TEN TOP TIPS!
## FOR GETTING STARTED IN CREATIVE WRITING

1 Write! Write! Write! Don't wait for inspiration but write something every day, even if it's a journal or just a shopping list.

2 Treat things that you read or see or hear as potential stories: a snippet in the newspaper, an item on the news, a conversation overhead on the bus, an unusual word.

3 Google 'creative writing exercises' – you'll be amazed at the variety on offer.

4 Join an online forum for writers, or look for blogs about writing.

5 Remember that writing should be fun, not a chore and not scary!

6 Look at your favourite magazine. If it has the kind of stories or articles or poems that you think you could write – have a go!

7 Decide what you want to write: is it a poem, a play, a story, a novel, a memoir. Then look at your favourite writers and be inspired by how they do it.

8 Keep a notebook handy… day dream… or note down your night dreams…

9 **JOIN A WRITING CLASS OR GROUP**

10 Try some of these writing exercises…

# FUN WRITING EXERCISES

Open a book or magazine and with your eyes closed, place your finger on the page. Write down the word it points to. Do this 5 times. Use whatever words you come up with to write a very short story or description

Take the first line of a novel – your favourite, one you are reading now, one you really disliked – and use it to start a totally different short story or poem.

Write a 26 line story or poem, where each sentence begins with the next letter of the alphabet (e.g. Alice was late. Before she started making her excuses she sat down. Clare, her friend, sighed…).

Play the old paper game 'Consequences' with one or more friends. Make up a story from the scenario you are left with – if it doesn't make sense, change anything you need to!

# MEET THE AUTHORS

### *R. Briden*

I'm from sunny South Carolina, but have enjoyed the green fields of Scotland for five years, and consider it home. Currently I'm working with children and youth for Calvary Chapel Edinburgh. It is my dream to complete my story "Neam" for my young friends, I hope you enjoy it.

### *Marie Campbell*

I live in Edinburgh with my partner and son, and am currently on a break from my job as a Civil Servant. I have always loved literature and started writing regularly around three years ago. I have written several short stories, some of which have been published or shortlisted in competitions. My first novel has just been accepted by an agent.

### *George Chalmers*

I am a retired social worker, a retired furniture-maker (first trade), a retired bank robber (second trade) and perpetual ex-con. I have been writing for various publications, mostly the Scottish Review, for twenty years or so. I won a few Koestler awards in prison and have been shortlisted for the Scottish Book Trust Award. Interests include keeping fit, movies with writing across the bottom and new innovations in balaclavas.

### *Coreen Connell*

Born in South Africa, brought up in Australia by Aberdonian parents, it's not much wonder I was a mixed up kid. We moved around so much that I didn't make many friends but had books, pen and paper as substitutes. Marrying and bringing up my own family in Scotland, I finally return to pen and paper. Thanks to the encouragement of the Gilmerton creative writing class members and tutor, I am happily back into writing.

### *Sheila Corrigan*

I am a senior citizen who acknowledges she is not as young as she used to be but not, perish the thought, growing old. Writing, especially in this group, I find enjoyably challenging. It takes me into another realm as I give my imagination free rein. We are never too old to learn and develop new interests!

### *Anne Hamilton*

For several years now I've enjoyed being a creative writing tutor online and at various writing classes around Edinburgh. I am a published writer and combine this with working as editor and mentor to other writers, and looking after my young son.

*Elizabeth Nallon*

I discovered creative writing in my middle years. At first it was a tentative journey but the support of the Gilmerton Writing Class has really helped. I've worked in offices most of my career so it's good to be able now to use words in a fun and creative way.

# AFTERWORD

We hope that these stories and poems have been as enjoyable to read as they were to write. If they, and some of the exercises we've included, have inspired you to think about doing some writing yourself, either as a complete beginner or someone who already has some experience, then why not think about joining us?

The Gilmerton Writing Group is an adult education class provided by Edinburgh City Council and offers a warm welcome to anyone interested in creative writing. We meet weekly, during term times, where we talk, write, read – and maybe even learn!

Gilmerton Community Centre, Drum Street

Tuesdays

2.30 – 4.30pm

Or contact Heather Muchamore, Community Learning and Development Tel 672 2516 or 07876791493 for more information.